HOW DID WE FIND OUT . . . SERIES
   Each of the books in this series on the history of science emphasizes the process of discovery.

"How Did We Find Out" Books by
Isaac Asimov

HOW DID WE FIND OUT THE EARTH IS ROUND?

HOW DID WE FIND OUT ABOUT ELECTRICITY?

HOW DID WE FIND OUT ABOUT NUMBERS?

HOW DID WE FIND OUT ABOUT DINOSAURS?

HOW DID WE FIND
ABOUT DINOSAU

HOW DID WE FIND OUT
ABOUT DINOSAURS?

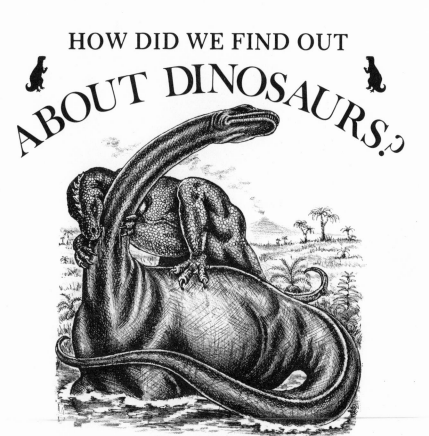

Isaac Asimov
Illustrated by David Wool

WALKER AND COMPANY
New York

To Marcia and Nick Repanes

First published in the United States of America in 1973 by the Walker
Publishing Company, Inc.

Published simultaneously in Canada by Fitzhenry & Whiteside, Limit-
ed, Toronto.

Trade ISBN: 0-8027-6133-X
Reinf. ISBN: 0-8027-6134-8
LIBRARY OF CONGRESS CATALOG CARD NUMBER 72-95793

PRINTED IN THE UNITED STATES OF AMERICA

CONTENTS

1 FOSSILS

IN ORDER TO UNDERSTAND how people found out about dinosaurs, we must learn about the strange stony bones men found in the earth.

Until about two hundred years ago, most people in Europe and America knew very little about ancient history. Most of what they knew came from the Bible.

It seemed to people who read the Bible that the earth was first formed about six thousand years ago. Then, about four thousand five hundred years ago, according to the Bible, there was a huge flood, which destroyed everything.

After that, the earth settled down to its present shape and different nations were established. About three thousand years ago, the kind of history began that we know about from sources other than the Bible.

That was what almost everybody thought until the end of the 1700s.

If earth were only in existence for six thousand years, we wouldn't expect much change in the kind of living things on it. The people that live today look just about the same as the statues the Greek people made two thousand years ago. They look just about the same as the people in the pictures of the ancient Egyptians four thousand years ago.

The kind of animals described in ancient writings are like the animals that live today—lions, elephants, sheep, goats, hawks, bees, and so on. The plants described by the ancients are the same as modern plants.

But then something came up that partly upset this view of the earth's having begun only a few thousand years ago. It was something that at first did not seem important at all—just some curious rocky objects that were dug out of the earth every once in a while.

People have always been digging in the earth, even thousands of years ago. It is in the earth that we find the ores from which we get useful metals.

Sometimes, while digging, people came across rocky forms that looked like bones or shells. But sometimes they didn't look like the bones or shells of any familiar animals.

What could be done about them? Those odd rocks weren't what the miners were looking for. They just tossed them to one side and went on with their digging.

The first person to look upon mining in a scientific way was a German named Georgius Agricola (uh-GRIK-uh-luh), who lived four hundred years ago. He spent most of his life working in mines and studying the minerals dug out of the earth.

FOSSIL FISH

One book he wrote, which appeared in 1546, was called *De Natura Fossilium*. This is Latin and means "About the Nature of Digging." In this book, Agricola called everything that was dug out of the earth a "fossil" (FOS-il), which comes from a Latin word meaning "to dig."

To Agricola, rocks of all kinds were fossils, even those odd rocks that looked like bones. Since then, for some reason, people have stopped using the word fossil *except* when describing the odd rocks that looked like bones or footprints or other traces left by animals of long ago.

Another scientist who lived in the 1500s was a Swiss named Konrad von Gesner (GES-ner). He wrote books in which he tried to talk about and describe everything in nature. Gesner was the first man to draw pictures of fossils.

Gesner didn't consider fossils important, however. To him, they were just rocks that happened to form in such a way that they looked like bones. He included them only because he included everything.

A hundred years later, an English naturalist, John Ray, went a step further. He was also interested in plants and animals and studied all the plants he could find from the time he was a boy. In 1660, he published his first book of plant descriptions and, for forty years, he kept writing more and more elaborate books on both plants and animals.

He wasn't content just to describe them the way Gesner did. He tried to put different animals and plants into groups. After all, some animals resemble other animals; some plants resemble other plants. Lions, tigers, and cats resemble each other. Foxes, wolves, and dogs resemble each other. Cattle, sheep, and goats all have hooves and eat grass and so resemble each other.

Ray got used to studying the details of animals and plants, since it was by little details that he could decide whether some of them might be grouped together or not.

When he studied fossils, he couldn't believe they had formed by accident and just happened to look like bones. He was used to looking at details and there were too many details in those bones that were the same as those found in real bones. It was too much to expect it had just happened.

In a book he wrote in 1691, Ray said that the fossils were all that were left of animals that had lived long ago. He was the first one to say that.

Furthermore, even though the details of the fossils showed that they had once been bones, they were not exactly like the bones of animals that Ray knew. (And he knew a great many.) Ray therefore concluded that the animals that had once had those bones were not quite like any animals that lived today. The animals that those fossils belonged to had all died out. They were "extinct."

That was also possible according to the notions people had in those days about ancient history. Suppose some animals hadn't survived the great flood. Maybe the fossils represented animals that had died in the flood and that was why they were extinct.

Living at the same time as Ray, however, was a Danish scientist, Nicolaus Steno (STAY-noh). Like Ray, he thought the fossils were parts of animals that had once been alive.

He found fossils, for instance, that looked exactly like the teeth of sharks. The similarity was so exact that the fossils just had to be shark's teeth and nothing else.

The fossil teeth were made out of stone, though. That meant that the material in the original teeth

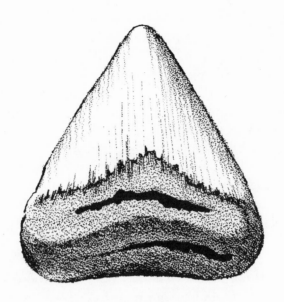

FOSSIL SHARK TOOTH

was slowly replaced, little by little, by minerals, as the teeth lay in the water.

But this new view posed a problem. If the stony fossils had once been bones, or teeth, or shells; and if the stone had formed little by little, that must have taken time. It must have taken a *lot* of time. Bones that have lain in the ground for hundreds of years don't even begin to turn to stone. It might take *millions* of years for this to happen.

In that case, then, how could the stony fossils have formed if the earth were only six thousand years old altogether? There wasn't enough time for fossils to form. Could it be that the earth was older than that?

Count de Buffon

During the 1700s, a few scientists began to wonder whether the earth might not be very old indeed. It wasn't easy to come right out and say that the earth was very old when the Bible seemed to say it wasn't.

The first person with the courage to advance a scientific theory about the age of the earth was a French naturalist, the Count de Buffon (boo-FON). In 1745, he suggested that the planets might have been formed when the sun collided with another large body. Pieces of matter were knocked out of the sun in the collision and became the planets.

How long would it take, Buffon wondered, for the earth to cool off, starting at the temperature of the sun? He calculated that it would take seventy-five thousand years. About forty thousand years ago, he decided, it became cool enough for living plants and animals to develop.

Many people were shocked at Buffon's theory because it didn't agree with the Bible. And yet even forty thousand years of life was not enough to explain the fossils. Not nearly enough. The earth and the life on it would have to be much older than that.

2
CATASTROPHES?

TWENTY YEARS AFTER BUFFON, a Swiss naturalist, Charles Bonnet (boh-NAY) thought he saw a way out. He could explain the fossils, allow the earth to be very old, and still not go against the Bible.

Suppose, he suggested, that the earth had existed for a long time. During that time, all kinds of living things might have existed on it. Then there would be some terrible event, some catastrophe or disaster, that would destroy all the life on earth.

For a while, the earth would remain dead, but the new kinds of life would form and again earth would go on for many thousands of years before some new huge catastrophe struck and destroyed life again. There might have been many such periods in the history of the earth.

The last disaster, Bonnet thought, could have taken place about six thousand years ago. All the living things on earth now, including human beings, would only have existed since then. In that case, the Bible would only deal with the last six thousand years. The earlier periods of earth's history would be ignored in the Bible.

Bonnet thought that the fossils were buried bits of ancient life that had existed in previous periods of earth's history, before the last catastrophe. Of course, they could be very old, tens and hundreds of thousands of years old, but that had nothing to do with Biblical history.

Bonnet's theory also explained the fact that although fossil bones resembled living bones, the resemblance wasn't exact. Why not? If the animals were from previous periods, why shouldn't they be different from those that live now?

A completely different theory was worked out by a Scottish scientist named James Hutton (HUT-on). He was not interested in fossils, as much as in the structure of the earth itself.

He noticed there were certain changes taking place on earth even as he watched. The rivers carried small quantities of salt to the ocean, so that the ocean was slowly getting saltier. Rivers also carried mud down to the ocean. This mud settled down at the bottom of the riverbed and at the bottom of that part of the ocean near the river's mouth. As more and more mud settled down, it got pressed together and hardened into a kind of rock.

Another kind of rock was produced when volcanoes sent out streams of molten lava. Solid rock formed when the lava cooled. Gradually, such rocks were built up into thick layers.

Rocks are not only formed, they are broken up. All kinds of rock are gradually broken into pieces by the

16

action of wind and running water. They become particles of sand and clay.

All these changes take place *very* slowly. Yet thick layers of rock were once slowly built up out of mud or lava. There are very large quantities of sand and clay that were formed very slowly from rock. For all that to happen from such slow changes meant the earth must be *very* old.

In 1785, Hutton published a book called *Theory of the Earth* in which he wrote about his views. He said the earth must be so old that he could see no signs of its beginning. What's more, he saw no reason for supposing there had been any catastrophes. He believed that the slow changes that were taking place in the present had always taken place in the past, and just as slowly.

By the end of the 1700s, then, more and more scientists were becoming convinced the earth was very old. But what kind of a history did it have? Was it full of catastrophes, as Bonnet suggested? Or was it a history of slow and steady change, as Hutton said?

For a while Hutton's theories made no impression and it was Bonnet's theory that was popular.

This was partly because Bonnet's theory could be made to fit the Bible. In addition, though, there were other arguments.

Have you ever passed a place where the side of a hill has been cut away so that a highway can be built? If so, you may have noticed that the rock forms different layers.

The first person who described these layers was Steno, who found the shark teeth fossils. About 1670,

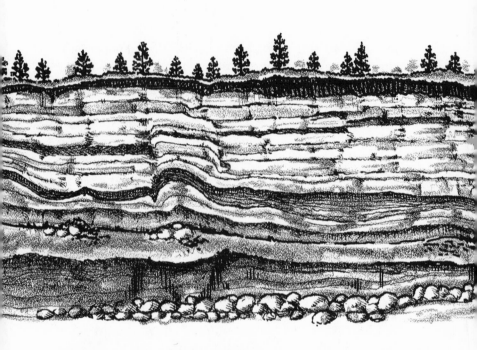

he was calling these layers of rock "strata" (STRAY-
tuh), which is the Latin word for "layers."

Nothing much was thought about the strata of
rock for over a hundred years after Steno had given
them the name. Then, in 1793, an Englishman, Wil-
liam Smith, was put in charge of having canals dug
in the English countryside.

D. WOOL

Many hills had to be cut in order to let the water of the canal flow through. Smith began to notice the strata of the exposed rock, as Steno had. Smith also noticed that the strata contained fossils. Furthermore, each layer had special kinds of fossils that were different from the fossils that were found in other layers.

Smith followed the strata and found that they often continued for long distances. They might be bent and broken here and there. In some places, they might even disappear because the action of wind and water had gradually worn them away. Then in another place, even miles away, the strata would show up again. There they would be, in the same order; and each of the strata with its particular kind of fossils.

All of this material appeared in 1816 in a book Smith published called *The Geological Map of England*.

It could be argued that the strata showed that Bonnet's theory of catastrophes was correct. Each layer was composed of mud that settled to the bottom of lakes or rivers and was squeezed down and hardened into rock. Maybe each layer was the result of millions of years of mud-settling. Then a catastrophe would come along and everything would start all over again. There would be a new layer formed of a different kind of mud, and each layer would naturally look a little different from the others.

Then, too, if there were different forms of life in each of the times between catastrophes, you would expect to find different fossils in each layer. You could identify a layer by the fossils it contained. Smith's discoveries would then make sense.

3 EVOLUTION

WHAT DO WE MEAN when we say that some fossils are different from others? The differences can be very small indeed. Before we can be sure about those differences, it is important to study living creatures in great detail. Then we can see how one plant or animal is different from another. We can see where there are small differences and where there are large ones. After that, we can study the fossils and see how they fit into the scheme.

A beginning was made by a Swedish naturalist named Carolus Linnaeus (lih-NEE-us). In 1735, he published a book in which he listed all the plants and animals he was able to study. He described them carefully and placed them in groups.

Each kind of plant or animals is a "species" (SPEE-sheez). Linnaeus placed species that resembled each other closely into a group called a "genus" (JEE-nus). He gave every plant or animal two Latin names, the first for its genus, the second for its species.

Lions, tigers, and cats are different species, but they are similar. They are all part of the genus *Felis* (FEE-lis), which is a Latin word for "cat." Linnaeus called the lion *Felis leo*, the tiger *Felis tigris*, and the cat *Felis domesticus*.

Just naming the species meant that each species had to be studied very carefully, so it could be put into the right genus.

Larger and larger groups could also be worked out. For example, all the species that have hair and are warm-blooded are "mammals" (MAM-ulz). You and I are mammals. Species that have feathers and are warm-blooded are "birds." Species that are covered with scales and breathe air are "reptiles" (REP-tilz). Species that are covered with scales and breathe water are "fish."

Mammals, birds, reptiles, and fish are similar in that they all have bones inside them. They are grouped together as "vertebrates" (VUR-tuh-brayts).

Linnaeus's system of placing species into larger and larger groups was improved by a French biologist, Georges Cuvier (koo-VYAY). Cuvier specialized in anatomy; in studying the shapes and forms of the bones and organs in a living animal. He used all the details in helping him group the species.

Beginning in the 1790s, Cuvier showed that different animals had characteristics that went along with each other. For example, horns and hooves went together with plant-eating. No meat-eating animal had horns or hooves. Meat-eating animals had certain kinds of teeth that plant-eating animals didn't have. Cuvier discovered one could tell a great

GEORGES CUVIER

deal about an animal from just a small part of its body; even from one tooth sometimes.

Cuvier divided plants and animals into very large groups, each of which he called a "phylum" (FI-lum). For instance, every animal that has a no-tochord, a rod of cells that forms the supporting axis of the body, is a member of a phylum called Chorda-ta (kawr-DAY-tuh). Any vertebrate such as man, an elephant, a snake, a frog, or a codfish is a member of this phylum. (The embryos of vertebrates have no-tochords which later become the spinal column.)

A butterfly, a spider, a lobster, and a centipede are all members of another phylum called Arthropoda (ahr-THROP-uh-duh), and so on.

Once Cuvier had his system worked out, he could apply it to fossils. He soon found out that the fossils were not completely different from living species.

Every fossil he studied turned out to belong to one phylum or another of those that exist today. There were fossils which were chordates, just as much chor-dates as you and I are. Other fossils were arthropods, and so on.

Of course, there were differences. A fossil might be a chordate yet not be exactly like a chordate alive today.

Cuvier found out something else about the fossils that were located in the various strata of rock.

Suppose that you cut into a hillside at a certain place and found five strata, one on top of the other. Naturally, you would expect the one at the bottom to be the oldest. It formed first, then another formed on top of it, and another on top of that. The one nearest

24

the surface would be the youngest. This meant the farther down the strata you found a fossil, the older it had to be.

Each one of the strata had its own kinds of fossils and Cuvier found that the fossils in the top one were the most similar to the kind of animals living today. The farther down the strata he looked, the more different the fossils were from living animals.

It was as though many millions of years ago, when the oldest strata were forming, living things were quite different from what they are now. There were slow changes with time so that animals and plants became more and more like present-day ones. By the time the topmost layer was formed, the animals and plants were almost as they are today.

This slow change in the nature of living species as time passes is called "evolution" (ev-oh-LYOO-shun).

Even though Cuvier's findings made it look as if evolution might have taken place, Cuvier didn't believe it had. Cuvier was sure that species didn't change. He felt, like Bonnet, that there had been catastrophes, and that after each catastrophe, new species formed. Each time new species formed, they would be more like modern forms, but there would be no connection between one set of species and the next.

As more and more fossils were studied, however, it became unlikely that a catastrophe had wiped out all life. Although different strata had different fossils for the most part, there were always a few of the same kinds of fossils that would appear in different strata.

This meant that these species lived on and became the ancestors of plants and animals in the next age.

For that reason, some scientists began to switch to Hutton's views of slow and steady change. The most important of these was a Scotsman, Charles Lyell (LY-ell).

Between 1830 and 1833, Lyell published three volumes of a book called *The Principles of Geology*, in which he carefully collected all evidence to show that catastrophes did not take place. He produced reasons for thinking that life had always existed on earth ever since the oldest fossils.

Lyell decided the oldest fossils were several hundred million years old. (Compare that with Buffon's figures of forty thousand years, less than a century before Lyell.) His book was so convincing that the notion of catastrophes killing all of life every once in a while during earth's history was abandoned.

Instead, from the 1830s on, people began to accept the idea that life had existed for hundreds of millions of years without ever being interrupted.

There had been scientists now and then, even in ancient times, who had speculated about evolution. The man who proved it, however, was an English naturalist, Charles Robert Darwin.

In 1831, Darwin went on a five-year cruise around the world and studied plants and animals everywhere he went. He took the first volume of Lyell's book with him and read it with great interest. In the course of the voyage, he saw for himself evidence of the great age of the earth. He found fossils that

CHARLES DARWIN

proved that animals were different in the past. He studied island life and figured out how species changed on islands because they became adapted to the special conditions on each island. He came to realize that plants and animals on earth were once quite different from those of today. They had slowly changed as time went on and gradually began to look like the ones we have around us. Finally, in 1859, he published a book called *The Origin of Species*, in which he carefully described all the evidence he could find.

Many people were shocked at Darwin and his book because they thought the whole notion of evolution went against the words of the Bible. Darwin's book was so carefully thought out, however, that evolution came to be accepted by scientists.

More and more evidence in favor of it was collected. Most of this evidence came from fossils, so let's go back to them.

4 the Ancient ANIMALS

WHEN CUVIER WAS WORKING ON FOSSILS, he was known as the great fossil expert. People who found interesting fossils often brought them to him.

For instance, a huge fossil claw was brought to him once. It had been found in America and there was a feeling it might be the claw of a giant lion now extinct.

Cuvier studied the claw carefully and saw that it was not like that of a lion, or of any meat-eating animal. In fact, it was like the claw of a sloth. Sloths are South American animals that live in trees and feed on leaves and twigs. They hang upside down, holding on to branches with their strong claws and move very slowly.

Cuvier decided that the claw he had belonged to a giant sloth. He was right. Other fossil finds showed that in the Americas there were once sloths so large they couldn't hang from branches. Some were 20 feet long and weighed as much as a modern elephant. Since animals that large had to live on the ground they were called "ground sloths." Their sci-

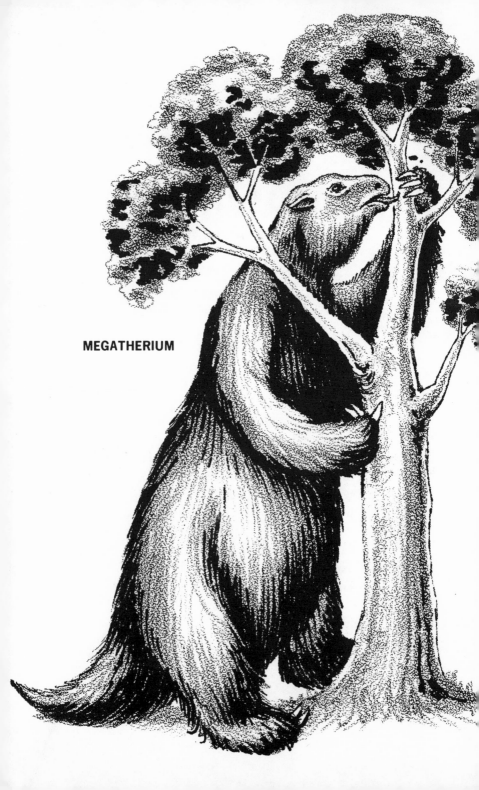

MEGATHERIUM

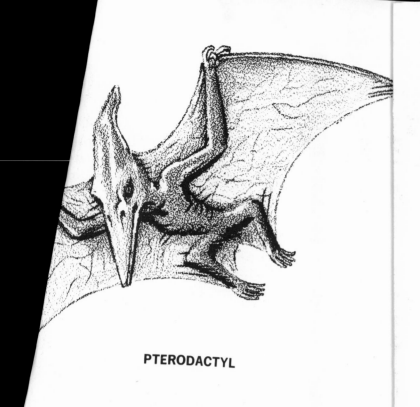

PTERODACTYL

large, but in later years the bones of much larger flying reptiles were found. The entire group was called *pterosaurs* (TER-uh-sawrz) which means "wing lizards."

Some of these had wings which, if stretched out as far as possible, were 25 feet from end to end. These were the largest flying animals that ever lived.

The year before Cuvier identified the pterodactyl, a twelve-year-old girl, Mary Anning, discovered a set of fossil bones of a large animal in a cliff near her home in southern England. The fossil bones stretched out for 30 feet.

entific name is *Megatherium* (meg-uh-THEE-ree-um), which means "large beast."

Some other large fossil bones were brought to Cuvier. There were not just claws; there were other bones as well.

Back in 1766, near the Meuse River in the Netherlands (a river called Mosa by the old Romans), there was a stone quarry. People dug out stones for building uses. While digging up rocks, some of the workers came upon some fossil bones.

Fortunately, someone in the nearby town knew about fossils and got them from the workers and saved them. Other bones were found, and, in 1780, a huge skull was located.

There was considerable argument as to what kind of an animal those bones represented. Eventually, in 1795, the fossil bones were sent to Cuvier.

This was where the careful study of detail came in. It is easy to tell a living mammal from a reptile because a mammal has hair and is warm-blooded, while a reptile has scales and is cold-blooded. But suppose all you have are some bones. Well, it turns out that mammals and reptiles have certain differences in their bones and an expert can tell them apart.

From the arrangement of bones in the skull, Cuvier could see at once that the fossil from the stone quarry was a reptile and not a mammal. (Lizards, snakes, turtles, and alligators are examples of reptiles that are alive today.) Cuvier decided the fossil skeleton was more like that of a lizard than anything else.

The leg bones of this ancient lizard were shaped in such a way that the legs must have been paddles. It

MOSASAUR

was a sea lizard and it eventually received the name of *Mosasaur* (MOH-zuh-sawr) meaning "Mosa-lizard." It was quite a large animal. Some fossils have been discovered that show the mosasaur to be up to 45 feet long, as large as a fairly big whale.

Cuvier had thus shown that in past ages there had lived both giant mammals and giant reptiles.

Naturally, people were excited by the thought that once long ago, huge monsters had lived on the earth. Could it be that ages ago cavemen had to fight such monsters? Was that where tales of giants, ogres, and dragons came from?

No, not really. It tu
mals came from very a
before there were any si
first appeared on earth al

Just the same way it
found by men in early tim
them the idea that giants,
existed.

It wasn't just the large siz
interesting. Cuvier heard of
that was quite small. It had
creatures with bones. In this c
legs seemed to be very long.

There were drawings of this
Cuvier studied them carefully. T
arrangement were just what you
reptile, but what about those funn
end of each of the forelegs were f
bones. Three of these were small a
the fourth and last set of finger bo
than all the rest of the arm. It was jus
on each forearm that made it so long.

Why should that one finger be so lo
to Cuvier that the finger could only be
had a web of skin attached to it. Such a
of skin would be a wing. In other words,
reptile he was studying had wings so it
been able to fly. Cuvier called it a *pterodac
uh-DAK-til), meaning "wingfinger."

Cuvier's find was a sensation. After all, th
such thing as a flying reptile alive today.

The first fossil, studied by Cuvier, was n

entific name is *Megatherium* (meg-uh-THEE-ree-um), which means "large beast."

Some other large fossil bones were brought to Cuvier. There were not just claws; there were other bones as well.

Back in 1766, near the Meuse River in the Netherlands (a river called Mosa by the old Romans), there was a stone quarry. People dug out stones for building uses. While digging up rocks, some of the workers came upon some fossil bones.

Fortunately, someone in the nearby town knew about fossils and got them from the workers and saved them. Other bones were found, and, in 1780, a huge skull was located.

There was considerable argument as to what kind of an animal those bones represented. Eventually, in 1795, the fossil bones were sent to Cuvier.

This was where the careful study of detail came in. It is easy to tell a living mammal from a reptile because a mammal has hair and is warm-blooded, while a reptile has scales and is cold-blooded. But suppose all you have are some bones. Well, it turns out that mammals and reptiles have certain differences in their bones and an expert can tell them apart.

From the arrangement of bones in the skull, Cuvier could see at once that the fossil from the stone quarry was a reptile and not a mammal. (Lizards, snakes, turtles, and alligators are examples of reptiles that are alive today.) Cuvier decided the fossil skeleton was more like that of a lizard than anything else.

The leg bones of this ancient lizard were shaped in such a way that the legs must have been paddles. It

MOSASAUR

was a sea lizard and it eventually received the name of *Mosasaur* (MOH-zuh-sawr) meaning "Mosalizard." It was quite a large animal. Some fossils have been discovered that show the mosasaur to be up to 45 feet long, as large as a fairly big whale.

Cuvier had thus shown that in past ages there had lived both giant mammals and giant reptiles.

Naturally, people were excited by the thought that once long ago, huge monsters had lived on the earth. Could it be that ages ago cavemen had to fight such monsters? Was that where tales of giants, ogres, and dragons came from?

No, not really. It turned out that such giant animals came from very ancient strata. They lived long before there were any signs of men. By the time men first appeared on earth all these monsters were gone.

Just the same way it may be that fossil bones found by men in early times were what helped give them the idea that giants, ogres, and dragons once existed.

It wasn't just the large size of the fossils that was interesting. Cuvier heard of a particularly old fossil that was quite small. It had the usual four legs of creatures with bones. In this case, though, the forelegs seemed to be very long.

There were drawings of this fossil and, in 1812, Cuvier studied them carefully. The bones and their arrangement were just what you would expect in a reptile, but what about those funny forelegs? At the end of each of the forelegs were four sets of finger bones. Three of these were small and ordinary, but the fourth and last set of finger bones was longer than all the rest of the arm. It was just the one finger on each forearm that made it so long.

Why should that one finger be so long? It seemed to Cuvier that the finger could only be that long if it had a web of skin attached to it. Such a thin stretch of skin would be a wing. In other words, the ancient reptile he was studying had wings so it must have been able to fly. Cuvier called it a *pterodactyl* (TER-uh-DAK-til), meaning "wingfinger."

Cuvier's find was a sensation. After all, there is no such thing as a flying reptile alive today.

The first fossil, studied by Cuvier, was not very

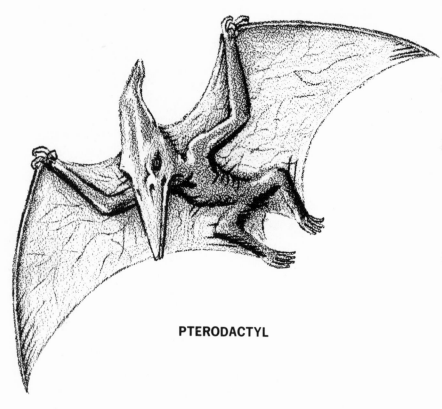

PTERODACTYL

large, but in later years the bones of much larger flying reptiles were found. The entire group was called
pterosaurs (TER-uh-sawrz) which means "wing
lizards."

Some of these had wings which, if stretched out as
far as possible, were 25 feet from end to end. These
were the largest flying animals that ever lived.

The year before Cuvier identified the pterodactyl,
a twelve-year-old girl, Mary Anning, discovered a set
of fossil bones of a large animal in a cliff near her
home in southern England. The fossil bones
stretched out for 30 feet.

ICHTHYOSAUR

The arrangement of the bones was similar to that of a fish. When the bones of the skull were studied closely, however, it turned out the animal wasn't a fish but a sea reptile. Cuvier helped draw that conclusion.

There are reptiles nowadays such as sea turtles and sea snakes. There is no reptile that has a shape like a fish, however. Mary Anning's fossil was named an *ichthyosaur* (IK-thee-uh-sawr), which means "fish lizard."

PLESIOSAUR

In 1821, Mary Anning (who made a profession of fossil hunting) discovered another sea reptile. This one had longer paddles than the mosasaur had, and it also had a very long neck. It was called *plesiosaur* (PLEE-see-uh-sawr) which means "almost-lizard." This is because it looked more like a reptile and less like a fish than the ichthyosaur did.

Cuvier wasn't always right. Sometimes he made mistakes.

In 1822, an English fossil hunter, Gideon Algernon Mantell, came across some teeth and bones which looked as though they belonged to an animal about 20 feet long.

He chipped a few teeth and bones out of the rock and sent them to Cuvier. Cuvier inspected them carefully and decided they were the remains of a large mammal. He thought the teeth were the teeth of a rhinoceros.

Mantell had no choice but to go along with Cuvier, who was the great expert. But then a couple of years later, he came across teeth that had come from the jaws of an iguana (ih-GWAH-nuh), a large lizard that lives in desert areas of North America.

The teeth were exactly like the teeth of his fossil, except that the fossil teeth were much larger. This meant that the fossil had to be a reptile. Mantell called his fossil an *Iguanodon* (ih-GWAH-nuh-don) meaning "iguana tooth." When Cuvier saw the iguana tooth, he, too, had to admit that Mantell was right.

The iguanodon, when it was alive, was like a huge, heavy kangaroo, covered with scales, and much larger than an elephant.

By the time the 1840s arrived, so many different fossil reptiles had been uncovered that they could be divided into different groups, according to the exact arrangement of the bones in their skulls. The ichthyosaurs belonged in one group all by themselves. The plesiosaurs belonged in another group. The pterosaurs were in a third group.

There was nothing particularly frightening about these creatures. The ichthyosaurs and plesiosaurs were sea creatures that couldn't climb onto land. If

IGUANODON

they lived today, they wouldn't harm man. The pterosaurs were flying creatures, mostly small, and probably less dangerous than eagles.

There were, however, two groups of land reptiles, with skull bones like those on the pterosaurs, which were much more frightening. Some of them were the largest meat-eating animals that ever lived on land. Compared to them, lions are kittens. Some of the plant-eating reptiles were even larger. Though they wouldn't have eaten us if we lived then, they could easily have crushed us without even noticing that there was a lump under their feet.

In 1842, these two groups of enormous reptiles were named *dinosaurs* (DIGH-nuh-sawrz), meaning "terrible lizards," by an English naturalist named Richard Owen.

The very first of the dinosaurs to be discovered was the iguanodon, and it was that one which Cuvier missed. With all his remarkable discoveries, he cannot be given credit for having discovered the first dinosaur. That credit goes to Mantell.

5 the REPTILES Develop

WHEN DARWIN'S BOOK ON EVOLUTION came out in 1859, people became even more interested in the dinosaurs and other extinct animals.

The dinosaurs weren't just large and curious creatures that had once lived and didn't live any more. They were part of a long history of developing and evolving life. The fossils of the giant reptiles were found in lower and older strata than the fossils of giant mammals. In fact, in the places where many reptile fossils could be found, there were no mammal fossils at all.

Was it possible that the reptiles were the most important living things on land at a time when there were no mammals? Did some reptiles gradually evolve into mammals? Were some extinct reptiles our own ancestors?

Ever since Darwin's time, fossil hunters have been working hard to find as many fossils as possible. They try to find out exactly how old the strata are in which particular fossils are found. They study the exact shape and all the details of the fossil to find out what kind of a plant or animal it was.

In this way, they get an idea of how life evolved. They learn how species very slowly changed over millions of years from one form to another.

In order to study the history of life, we must begin with the oldest strata that have fossils. It wasn't until 1907 that scientists learned to work out the age of these strata by the way certain chemicals slowly changed in the rock. They knew how fast the chemicals changed, and how much change had taken place. From that they could calculate the age of the rock.

It turned out that the oldest fossils were in rocks that were six hundred million years old. Even those oldest fossils are the remains of quite complicated animals, however. There must have been many more hundreds of millions of years of life before that. It's just that the very early life had soft bodies and lacked bones or shells that could be easily fossilized.

The oldest fossils that have been found are of different kinds of sea creatures—many shellfish, for instance. All the phyla that exist today, except one, existed six hundred million years ago.

This one exception is the chordate phylum, to which the reptiles and mammals belong. The first chordate fossils appear in strata that are about five hundred million years old. By the time another hundred million years had passed, fish-like chordates were common.

But even the chordates, when they first developed, were all sea creatures. Until about four hundred

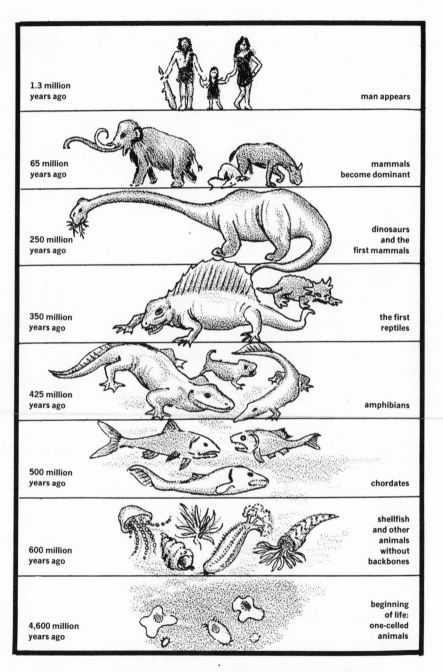

1.3 million years ago	man appears
65 million years ago	mammals become dominant
250 million years ago	dinosaurs and the first mammals
350 million years ago	the first reptiles
425 million years ago	amphibians
500 million years ago	chordates
600 million years ago	shellfish and other animals without backbones
4,600 million years ago	beginning of life: one-celled animals

HOW LIFE DEVELOPED ON THE EARTH

twenty-five million years ago, the land surface of the earth had no visible life on it. There may have been bacteria in the soil, but there were no plants and no animals.

There were living creatures in the ocean, though. When the tide went out, some were trapped on dry land for awhile. Slowly, those animals that could best withstand the dry period survived more frequently and reproduced more young like themselves. Gradually, in the course of millions of years, living things changed in such ways as to survive on dry land for longer and longer times.

Plants began to live on the land, too. The small animals that became adapted to dry land, such as spiders, insects, and snails, could feed on the dry-land plants, and these populated the continents, too.

Chordates also found themselves trapped on dry land when the tide went out. Or else they lived in small lakes that sometimes dried up in hot weather. This meant that they would have to flop overland to another lake. The chordates that were best at this were certain fish with strong fins. They could flop around on land, supported on those fins.

As millions of years passed, the fins developed into actual legs and the fish started to breathe air. They laid eggs, however, that had no protection. Those eggs had to be laid in water or they would dry out and die. The little creatures that came out of the eggs had to continue living in water until they became adults. Then they developed legs and could come out on land.

Such animals which live in water when young and

on land when grown, are called *amphibians* (am-FIH-bee-unz), meaning "double life." The best known amphibian alive today is the frog. It lays its eggs in water. These hatch out into tadpoles which live in water. Finally, the tadpoles develop lungs and legs and come onto land.

About three hundred fifty million years ago, the largest living things on land were amphibians. They weren't little frogs, though. They were powerful creatures that looked a little like alligators. Some were 10 or 15 feet long.

These amphibians had to live near water, however, so they could lay their eggs there. When those eggs hatched, the tiny young that came out had to continue to live in water and were quite helpless and unprotected for a while.

Then another change took place. Some of the amphibians were developing eggs that were better and better protected. Some were laid with shells that kept water inside so that the eggs would not dry up. They let air through so the developing young could breathe.

This meant the eggs could be laid on land. They could be placed in protected places where they might be safe. The developing young could grow inside the egg till it filled it. By that time, it was grown enough to have legs and lungs and to be able to live on land.

Animals with such eggs didn't have to return to water to lay them. They were the first reptiles.

Those first reptiles were small. Because they weren't confined to water, however, and because their eggs were kept safe, they multiplied quickly. They spread overland to places the amphibians could not reach. The reptiles became the most important forms of life on land.

HEN'S EGG

FOSSIL DINOSAUR EGG

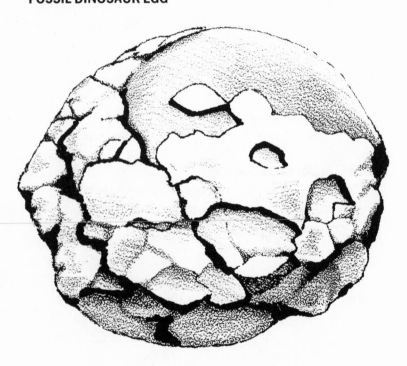

6 the Age of the DINOSAURS

BY TWO HUNDRED FIFTY MILLION YEARS AGO, the reptiles were all over the face of the land. Some had even returned to the sea, like the ichthyosaurs and plesiosaurs.

Others remained on land and by two hundred twenty-five million years ago, those reptiles we call dinosaurs first developed. By two hundred million years ago, the dinosaurs had become the most common type of reptile. They were divided into two groups. One group had hipbones a little like those of modern lizards and they were called *saurischians* (saw-RIS-kee-uns) meaning "lizard hips." The other had hipbones a little like those of modern birds and they were called *ornithischians* (awr-nih-THIS-kee-uns) meaning "bird hips."

The early dinosaurs were lizard-like animals that ran on their hindlegs. They had long tails to balance the forepart of the body. The forelegs were small and probably were used to clutch their food. Possibly they could run faster on two legs and this gave them an advantage in catching animals if they were meat

TYRANNOSAURUS

eaters, or getting away from animals chasing them if they were plant eaters.

Some of the saurischian dinosaurs grew into larger and larger species until about a hundred million years ago, when the *Tyrannosaurus* (tih-ran-uh-SAWR-us) developed. Its name means "master lizard." It looked something like a tremendous kangaroo. From the top of its head to the tip of its tail it was nearly 50 feet long. Its head, which was 6 feet long and armed with six-inch teeth, was nearly 20 feet above the ground. It was taller than a giraffe! It weighed up to 12 tons and was larger than the largest elephant!

DIPLODOCUS

The Tyrannosaurus and other dinosaurs like it are the largest meat-eating animals that ever lived on land.

Some of the saurischian dinosaurs were plant eaters, and plant eaters were usually larger than meat eaters. The plant-eating dinosaurs grew so large they couldn't support themselves on two legs. They had to use the forelegs, too, and the largest ones had to stay on all fours all the time. They had huge, thick legs, like beams.

One of them was the *Diplodocus* (dih-PLOD-uh-kus). The name means "double beam" because that's what the forelegs and hindlegs looked like. The di-

BRONTOSAURUS

plodocus had a long, thin neck, with a small head at the top. At the other end was a long, thin tail. In between was a thick body and four thick legs. It was up to 90 feet long from nose to tail tip, and was the longest land animal that ever lived.

A similar dinosaur was the *Brontosaurus* (bron-tuh-SAWR-us), a name that means "thunder lizard" because its footsteps may have sounded like thunder. It wasn't as long as the diplodocus, but it was stockier

BRACHIOSAURUS

and heavier. It probably weighed about 30 tons, three times as much as the largest elephant.

The heaviest of all was the *Brachiosaurus* (bray-kec-uh-SAWR-us), or "arm lizard." It is called that because its forelegs are particularly long for a dinosaur. It had a long neck and a rather short tail. It was very stocky and weighed up to 50 tons, so that it was the heaviest land animal that ever lived.

These large dinosaurs are the ones people know

best. When you see a picture of a dinosaur, it is very likely that of the brontosaurus.

The fossil skeletons of these really large dinosaurs in the 1870s were the most exciting dinosaur discoveries made. The man who made these discoveries was an American fossil hunter named Charles Othniel Marsh. He discovered eighty new kinds of dinosaurs altogether. Another dinosaur finder of the time was Edwin Brinker Cope. Marsh and Cope fought continually over who found the bones of the dinosaur first.

Some of the other group of dinosaurs, the ornithischians, also ran around on their two hindlegs. They include the iguanodons, for instance, which were the first dinosaurs to be discovered.

Other members of this group survived by developing thick, bony plates that were hard to bite through, as well as spikes and horns to strike back with. The best known examples of this type were also found by Marsh.

One of these is the 20-foot-long *Stegosaurus* (steg-uh-SAUR-us), a name that means "roof lizard." The reason it got that name is that among its fossil bones were a number of flat bones. At first the fossil experts thought the flat bones were laid down over the back of the animal like roof tiles to protect it from its enemies. A more careful study of the details of the bones showed that the flat bones stood up on end in a double row on each side of the backbone.

The stegosaur also had long spikes at the end of its tail. It was a plant eater, but with those bones on the back and the spikes on its lashing tail, it must have

STEGOSAURUS

been hard for a meat eater to get near it.

None of the dinosaurs had large brains. The stegosaur had a particularly small one. Though it was larger than an elephant, its brain was no larger than that of a kitten.

Another armored dinosaur is the *Triceratops* (try-SEH-ruh-tops), which means "three-horn face." It

TRICERATOPS

protected itself with its head, since the skull had a huge, bony frill that extended back over its neck. Over its eyes were two long horns, and on the nose was a third. It was up to 20 feet long. The triceratops was a plant eater and lived at the same time as the tyrannosaur. Even the great savage tyrannosaur probably seldom tackled a triceratops, however, or even got within reach of those horns.

The most thoroughly protected dinosaur was the

ANKYLOSAURUS

Ankylosaurus (ANK-ih-luh-sawr-us) which means "growing-together lizard." It is called this because all the bony plates fitted together to form a solid armor over its back. There were huge spikes on both sides of this back armor. The armor and spikes went right down the tail, and the end of the tail was formed into a huge, bony club. The ankylosaurus was practically a living tank.

Not all these dinosaurs lived at the same time, of

course. Some developed and continued to exist for several million years, then died out and became extinct. Dinosaurs of other types then took their place.

For instance, the stegosaur lived about one hundred fifty million years ago. It did well for millions of years, but then the ankylosaur and the triceratops developed. They were better protected than the stegosaur and had better brains. The stegosaur couldn't compete and died out.

And then, about seventy million years ago, *all* the dinosaurs died. Nobody knows what happened. There are many theories. Perhaps the climate changed. Perhaps other animals ate the dinosaur eggs. Perhaps something happened that we haven't guessed yet. No one knows!

We do know they all died. There is a layer of strata that still has fossils of the dinosaurs that developed in the last stages, like the tyrannosaur and the triceratops. And the layer above that has no dinosaur fossils at all. Not only did the dinosaurs disappear, but also other large reptiles such as the plesiosaurs and the ichthyosaurs. The winged pterosaurs also died, and some important groups of animals that weren't reptiles at all.

Why this happened is the biggest mystery in the story of evolution.

7 After the DINOSAUR

OF COURSE, NOT ALL THE REPTILES VANISHED. Some members of the class to which the two groups of dinosaurs belonged kept on living. The alligators and crocodiles of today are descended from them. Alligators and crocodiles are not dinosaurs but they are the closest surviving relatives of the dinosaurs.

The turtle family, which is even older than the dinosaurs continued to survive, too. The snakes and lizards also survived.

Then, again, some of the reptiles changed during the time when the dinosaurs ruled the land. They stopped being reptiles altogether.

About one hundred fifty million years ago, some of the smaller reptiles developed scales that didn't stick close to the body but that spread out and became frayed. They became feathers. In 1860, a fossil mark was found that looked just as though it had been made by a feather. The discoverer was a German fossil hunter, Hermann von Meyer. He called the animal that had owned the feather, *Archaeopteryx* (ahrkee-OP-tuh-rix), meaning "ancient wing."

57

ARCHAEOPTERYX

Later that same year, a fossil skeleton was found with more feather markings in the stone. The fossil was of a bird, but it had some reptile characteristics. It had teeth in its jaw, which no modern bird has. It had claws sticking outside the wing, like a pterodactyl did. The tail was like that of a lizard instead of a bird.

This was a very important find. Many people who objected to evolution said, "If some life-forms change into other life-forms, why don't we ever find any in which the change has gone only halfway?"

The archaeopteryx was just such a find. It was

about halfway between a reptile and a bird. It had characteristics of each. It showed that birds developed from reptiles. When the dinosaurs and other large reptiles died off, many birds survived, and from them have come all the modern birds.

Then, too, there were some early reptiles that developed teeth which were more complicated than those of most reptiles. Their teeth were like those of mammals today. They developed other characteristics similar to those of modern mammals.

Some of these reptiles (which were *not* dinosaurs, by the way) had developed hair and became true mammals. During all the time the dinosaurs ruled the earth, mammals also existed, but they were small and unimportant animals then.

However, when the dinosaurs and the other reptiles all died, the small mammals were among the animals that survived.

Without competition from the reptiles, they developed into all kinds of species. Some of them, like the megatherium, which Cuvier had identified, were quite large.

The largest land mammal that ever lived was the *Baluchitherium* (ba-loo-kih-THEE-ree-um) meaning "beast from Baluchistan," since that was where the fossil was found. It was a kind of rhinoceros that lived about thirty million years ago. The top of its shoulder was about 18 feet from the ground and it could raise its head to a point 27 feet from the ground. It weighed 20 tons, twice as much as an elephant. Still, it weighed less than half as much as the largest dinosaur.

BALUCHITHERIUM

But many of the large mammals died out, too. Around ten million years ago, some of the smaller mammals that had developed into ape-like animals were doing very well. From them, finally, apes and creatures like human beings developed. These are called *hominids* (HOM-ih-nidz).

Over the last million years, hominids developed into species that looked more and more the way we do today. Finally, a species developed that looked just the way we do.

This most recent species of hominid is called "Homo sapiens" (HOH-mo-SAY-pee-ens), meaning "man, the wise." It is the only species of hominid that now exists on the earth, and it includes you and me.

But of all the species who have lived on earth all these hundreds of millions of years, the most fascinating except for man himself are those giant dinosaurs.

INDEX